Making Homemade SOAPS & CANDLES

by PHYLLIS HOBSON

A Garden Way Guide
of HOMESTEAD RECIPES

GARDEN WAY PUBLISHING
CHARLOTTE, VERMONT, 05445

Library of Congress Catalog Card Number: 74-75461
ISBN 0-88266-026-8
COPYRIGHT 1974 BY GARDEN WAY PUBLISHING CO.

Drawings and Typography by Frank Lieberman

PRINTED IN THE UNITED STATES

MAKING YOUR OWN
SOAPS AND CANDLES

The art of making soap and candles so closely follows the history of our country that we can almost read the character of the times and the people by asking what they did with surplus animal fats.

The first colonists brought their soap kettles with them and at butchering time they made soap and candles in groups of families for all to share. As civilization crept in and the cities and towns developed, butchering was taken over by those who were paid for the task. Families put away their soap kettles and bought the hard yellow bars at the store along with the family food staples. The candles were replaced by kerosene and then electricity.

But as the West was opened and families set out to homestead lands far from the cities, once again they raised and butchered their own animals and made their own soap.

For the homesteaders, soapmaking was a symbol of self support, but many rural families — those that took pride in independence and abhorred waste — made their own soap well into the 20th Century.

Then during World War II, when animal fat was used to the utmost and commercial soap was in short supply, many American women once again displayed their independent spirit, looked up Grandmother's old recipes and revived the art of making soap and candles, this time on modern kitchen stoves.

And now we have come full circle. The new homesteaders, many of whom commute to town but work to make a small plot of land self-supporting, are making soap and candles — converting waste animal fat into useful products.

Others who live in town but share the same concern for the land, prefer the old soaps to the newer phosphate detergents. Still others find pleasure in preserving these almost-forgotten arts.

To yesterday's homesteader, animal fat was an important by-product of butchering. He raised his own meat and butchered it himself, saving every scrap of the animal for home use. The meat was dried and cured and canned. The hide was tanned. The head and intestines were saved for sausage. The fat was used for cooking and, just as important, for making soap and candles.

Today's homesteader may raise his own meat, but he usually has it butchered and packaged at the local meat locker and doesn't realize how much of the animal is being wasted. From even a small, fairly lean calf a butcher trims and discards 50 to 100 pounds of fat, which could be rendered into a pure white, hard tallow. Larger, fatter animals will provide even more.

This tallow can be converted into enough soap to last a family until the next butchering time. It also may be used to make candles. We've included recipes for both.

In addition to tallow, leftover kitchen grease which is unfit for anything else can be used for soap-making. Different kinds of fats may be mixed, and even strong-smelling or rancid grease will make perfectly good, sweet-smelling soap.

Candles require clean, hard fat — preferably beef tallow which produces a harder, cleaner-smelling candle. Properly made homemade candles have no offensive odor.

Many of the enclosed recipes are more than a century old and a few date back more than 200 years. To preserve their character we have retained the original wording as much as possible.

Some of the methods no longer may be practical, and a few of the recipes have been included as oddities. Wherever possible, we have clarified terms and simplified methods, but some of the ingredients no longer may be available, and you may find it necessary to make substitutions or improvise methods in some cases.

For practicality, a few modern recipes such as Simple Kitchen Soap and Boiled Kitchen Soap have been included.

MAKING SOAP

Making soap is one of the few ways a person with no special talent literally can "make something out of nothing". It also is a thrifty way to make good use of an otherwise wasted by-product of meat. It can be one's personal contribution toward cleaning our polluted waters by eliminating one major source of the phosphate from today's detergents.

With a few simple kitchen tools, ingredients you probably already have on hand and a few hours' work, you can make a month's supply of cleaning soap. It's a good idea to make soap once or twice a year because soap, like wine, improves with age.

The simplest and cheapest type is plain yellow laundry soap, the kind that made Grandmother's sheets so sparkling white. But with the addition of a few inexpensive ingredients you can create fine toilet soaps too.

The other ingredients are used to make soap clean better, to soften the water or to perfume the product. Most of them are available at grocery or drug stores. A few, such as the essences and oils used in scented toilet soaps, can be purchased in hobby shops which carry supplies for making soaps and candles.

Powdered borax is sold in grocery stores as a water softener. Potash lye is on the same shelf labeled "drain cleaner". Quick lime or ground limestone may be found in garden supply shops. Most drug stores carry resin or will order it for you.

The instructions are simple. Most of the ingredients are readily available. It's even possible to get some of them free of charge. Try making your own soap. You'll find it's fun, but be careful.

CAUTION!!!

Commercial lyes, potash lye and soda lye — even dampened wood ashes — are extremely caustic and can cause burns if splashed on the skin. They could cause blindness if spattered in the eye.

Use caution when adding lye to cold water, when stirring lye water and when pouring the liquid soap into molds. If it is spilled on the skin, wash off immediately with cold water. Wash off any lye or green (uncured) soap spilled on furniture or counter tops.

Though some of the old recipes didn't say so, always add lye to cold water, never to hot water, because the chemical action heats the cold water to the boiling point. It also produces harsh fumes which are harmful if breathed deeply. Stand back and avert the head while the lye is dissolving. The use of a draft vent is recommended.

Because of these dangers, it is best to keep small children from the room while soap is being made.

A container — A large iron soap kettle or a common wash boiler is great for making soap in large quantities over an open fire the way Grandmother made it. For indoor soap-making in smaller quantities, pots that are granite or porcelain-covered are the best to use because of the corrosive character of some of the recipes' ingredients. Dispose of soap-making wastes carefully outdoors, not in the drain. Never put lye or fresh soap in aluminum pans.

To make our Simple Kitchen Soap, melt the fat over low heat, then add it to the cooled lye water in a heavy crock. No cooking is required.

A Ladle — If an iron kettle is used a long-handled wooden ladle is needed to stir the soap. For indoor soap-making a wooden spoon will do. Once again — don't use aluminum.

A Grater or Grinder — A kitchen grater or a meat grinder is needed to make soap flakes for laundry use or to grind soap for some of the later recipes.

Molds — Grandmother used flat wooden boxes or wooden tubs to mold the soap while it cooled and hardened. Over the wood she laid pieces of cloth to keep the soap from sticking to the wood. You can buy fancy molds in hobby shops, but for home use discarded plastic bottles work just as well and are much cheaper.

A Plate — Some recipes call for a plate on which to cool a few drops of the liquid from time to time to test for doneness. Grandmother preferred a glass plate because it cooled the liquid faster.

THE INGREDIENTS

There are only three ingredients in plain soap — animal fat, lye and water. Any other ingredients are to improve the cleaning power, give the soap skin-softening qualities or give it a pleasant odor or color.

All three of the vital ingredients can be obtained free if you're willing to spend time instead of money. Unwanted fat scraps often are free for the asking at butcher shops or butchering plants. Just tell them what you want it for. A few hours over low heat (wood for an outdoor fire often is free for the chopping) and you have all the fat needed for a year's supply of soap.

And save the ashes from that fire. You'll need them to make the lye — also free. For recipes that call for soft water use rain water, chemically softened water or borax added to tap water.

TO PREPARE TALLOW OR GREASE

Cut up beef suet, mutton tallow or pork scraps and fry over low heat. Strain the melted grease through a coarse cloth and squeeze as much grease as possible out of the scraps. If you have an old lard press, it was made for this step.

Now clean the melted fat by boiling it in water to which a tablespoon of salt or alum has been added. Add twice as much water as fat and boil 10 minutes. Stir thoroughly and allow to cool. When the fat is cold it will have formed a hard cake on top of the water. Lift off the cake of fat and scrape the underside clean. Weigh and melt down according to the recipe.

TO MAKE POTASH LYE FROM ASHES

Fit a 50-gallon barrel or tub (only wood will do) with a faucet near the bottom, and make a filter inside around the mouth of the faucet with several bricks or stones covered with straw. Fill the tub with wood ashes. Ashes from oak wood make the strongest lye and those from apple wood make the whitest soap.

When the tub is full pour boiling water over the ashes until water begins to run from the faucet. Then shut the faucet and let the ashes soak. As they settle, add more ashes until the tub is full again.

The longer the water stands before being drawn off the stronger the lye will be. Usually a few hours will be enough. The strength of the lye need not always be the same, since in the soap-making the alkali will unite only with a certain proportion of fat, and more lye can be added until all the fat is saponified. Lye that will float a fresh egg is standard strength for soap-making.

If you do not have a big barrel or do not want that large a quantity, you may use a porcelain-covered or plastic pail. Fill the pail with ashes and add boiling water, stirring to wet the ashes. The ashes will settle to less than one-fourth their original volume. Add ashes to the top of the pail, stir again and let stand for 12 to 24 hours, or until the liquid is clear. Then carefully pour, dip or siphon off the clear liquid.

A GLOSSARY OF INGREDIENTS

Lye, Lye Water, Potash Lye (sometimes termed Caustic Potash Lye) — are made from steeped (slaked) wood ashes and are interchangable terms.

Potash (sometimes called Caustic Potash) — is lye water evaporated to a powder.

Lime (or Stone Lime) — is ground or agricultural limestone.

Quicklime — is lime that has been baked.

Soda Lye — is quicklime slaked in water and heated with sal soda.

Sal Soda — is hydrated sodium carbonate.

Caustic Soda — is soda lye evaporated to a powder.

Commercial Lye — usually is the same as caustic soda and is the equivalent of "lye" in most recipes.

TO MAKE POTASH

Potash may be made by boiling down the lye water in a heavy iron kettle. After the water is driven off there will remain a dark, dry residue which is known as "black salts". The heat must be maintained until this is melted, when the black impurities will be burned away and a grayish-white substance will remain. This is potash. Save what you don't use for the next time you make soap.

TO MAKE SODA LYE

Slake 1 quart of quicklime with 3 quarts water, which will reduce the lime to the consistency of cream. Dissolve 3 quarts sal soda in 5 quarts boiling water. Add the slaked lime, stirring vigorously. Keep the mixture at a boil until the ingredients are thoroughly mixed.

Allow the mixture to cool and settle, then pour off the lye liquid and discard the dregs in the bottom. Caustic soda may be produced from this liquid by boiling down the lye until the water is evaporated, and a dry residue is left in the kettle.

COMMERCIAL LYE

Most commercial lyes are caustic soda. One can of commercial lye may be substituted for the one pound of lye called for in most of the following recipes.

THE METHODS

To make any soap it is necessary to dilute lye, then mix it with fat or oil and stir until saponification takes place.

Saponification is the chemical reaction by which the two ingredients — lye water and fat — are converted into one substance — soap.

12

Soft soaps have saponified when they are thick and creamy, with a slightly slimy texture. They do not harden and are ready to use at this stage.

Uncooked hard soaps are ready to be poured into molds when the emulsion has thickened to the consistency of honey. Boiled hard soaps have saponified when the mixture is thick and ropy and slides off the spoon.

If lye water and fat are mixed when they are cold, the process of saponification may require several days or even months, depending upon the strength and purity of the ingredients. But if the temperature is raised to 212 degrees, the process of saponification will take place in a few minutes or few hours.

These are the two methods of making soap: the cold process and the boiling process. We've included both methods in the recipes for two different, but similar products, soft soap and hard soap.

SOFT SOAP

COLD PROCESS One of the simplest of the old, traditional recipes for homemade soap calls for 12 pounds of fat, 9 pounds of potash and 12 gallons of water.

Put the fat in a tight cask or barrel and add the potash which has been dissolved in 3 gallons of water. Once a day for the next 3 days add 3 gallons boiling water and stir vigorously for about 3 minutes. With a long stick or paddle kept in the mixture stir it several times a day.

In a month or so the soap will be free from lumps and will have a uniform jelly-like consistency. When stirred it will have a silky luster and will trail off in slender threads from the paddle, and then the soap is ready to use. It should be kept in a covered container.

MORE RECIPES FOR SOFT SOAP— COLD PROCESS

Mix in a kettle or wash boiler 8 pounds of melted grease with 18 quarts of strong lye water that will float a fresh egg. Bring to a boil, pour into the soap barrel and thin with weak lye water obtained by leaching wood ashes. Place the barrel out of doors in a warm place. The soap should be ready to use in a few weeks.

OR

Mix 10 pounds clear, melted grease, 6 pounds sal soda and 8 gallons hot water in the soap barrel. Stir once a day and let the mixture stand until completely saponified.

OR

Melt 8 pounds grease in a kettle and bring to the boiling point. In another kettle melt 8 pounds caustic soda and 1 pound sal soda in 4 gallons soft water. Pour all together into a 40-gallon cask. Fill up the cask with soft water, stir daily and let the mixture stand until saponified.

OR

Mix 6 pounds potash, 4 pounds lard and ¼ pound powdered rosin and allow the mixture to stand for one week. Then melt in a kettle with 2 or 3 gallons of water. Pour the mixture into a 10-gallon cask filled with soft water and stir two or three times a day for two weeks.

OR

Put into a kettle ¾ pound sal soda and 1 pound brown soap cut into shavings. Add 12 quarts of cold water, melt over low heat and stir until dissolved. It is ready for use as soon as it is cool.

BOILING PROCESS

Soft soap also may be made by boiling diluted caustic potash lye or lye from leached ashes with grease until saponification takes place. To do this put the grease in the soap kettle, add sufficient lye water in which to melt the grease without burning and continue to ladle in additional lye until all the grease is saponified. This will happen more quickly if the lye water is hot.

If too much lye is added the soap will have strong caustic properties. Then more grease must be added to take up the excess lye.

As the lye is added gradually and combined with the grease, the thick liquid will become stringy and turbid. It will fall from the paddle with a shining luster. A ladleful of lye should be added at regular intervals until the liquid becomes clarified in a uniformly clear slime.

To test for doneness put a few drops from the middle of the kettle on a plate to cool. If the soap remains clear when cool it is done. If there is a great deficiency of lye the drop of soap will be weak and gray. If the deficiency is not so great there may be a gray margin around the outside of the drop. If too much lye has been added a gray skin will spread over the whole drop. It will not be sticky, but while wet can be

slid easily along the plate. In this case the soap is overdone and more grease must be added.

The froth that rises as the mixture cooks is caused by an excess of water, and the soap must be kept on the fire until this is evaporated. Beat the froth with the paddle to admit air. When the froth ceases to rise, the soap falls lower in the kettle and takes on a darker color. White bubbles appear on the surface, one over the other, with a peculiar sound. The soap is "talking". It is ready for use.

MORE RECIPES FOR SOFT SOAP— BOILING PROCESS

Dissolve 8 pounds potash in a large iron pot with 3 or 4 gallons water brought to a boil. Melt 8 pounds clarified fat to the boiling point in a separate vessel. Put 4 gallons boiling water in a soap barrel and add first 1 quart hot fat and then 1 quart hot lye. Continue this — one stirring briskly while another adds ingredients — until fat and lye are all used.

Now pour in enough boiling water to fill the barrel, stirring constantly until the whole becomes a creamy emulsion with a uniform appearance. Let the barrel stand two months in a cool place til completely saponified.

OR

Dissolve 1 pound potash in 1 gallon cold water. Let it stand overnight and in the morning bring to a boil and add

10 ounces pure, clarified melted grease. Place this in a tub with 1½ gallons warm water. Mix well and allow to stand until saponified.

OR

Melt 4 pounds clear fat in one kettle and dissolve 4 pounds caustic potash in 6 quarts cold water in another. Pour 2 gallons soft water, boiling hot, into a clean tub or barrel and ladle into this the melted fat and the dissolved potash alternately, one person ladling and another stirring, until the ingredients are thoroughly mixed. Add boiling water each day, 2 gallons at a time, stirring vigorously each time, until it equals 16 gallons. Place the barrel in a cellar or other cool place and occasionally stir it for three minutes.

OR

Hard soap may be reduced to the consistency of soft soap by dissolving it in water. Shave the hard soap fine or run it through a meat grinder. Add twice its bulk of soft water and simmer with gentle heat until the soap is dissolved or let stand in cold water two or three days.

HARD SOAP

The old-fashion method of making hard soap is similar to that of making soft soap by boiling, but with the additional steps taken to separate water, glycerin, excess alkali and other impurities from the true soap.

This method requires three kettles — two small kettles to hold the lye and the fat respectively and one large enough to contain both ingredients without boiling over.

Put the clean, grained fat or the grease in one of the smaller kettles with enough water or weak lye to prevent burning, and raise the temperature to a boil. Put the lye water or a solution of sal soda or potash or both in the other small kettle and dissolve in boiling water.

Place the large kettle on the fire and ladle into it about one-fourth of the melted fat. Add an equal quantity of the hot lye, stirring the mixture constantly. Continue this way, one person ladling and another stirring, until about two-thirds of the fat and lye have been mixed thoroughly together.

At this stage the mixture should be a uniform emulsion of about the consistency of cream. A few drops of fluid cooled on a glass plate should show neither globules of oil nor water separately. A drop of the cooled liquid on the tongue should not have an alkaline, biting taste.

Now add enough strong lye to complete the decomposition of the fats and the removal of the glycerin. Continue boiling until the mixture has a strong alkaline or burning taste. Add the remainder of the fat and lye alternately, taking care that in the end there shall be no excess lye.

Up to this point the process is similar to boiling soft soap, and it is only necessary to evaporate the excess water by a boiling-down process.

The important difference in making hard soap is the addition at this point of salt. This is the means by which the creamy emulsion of oils and alkali is broken up. The salt has a stronger affinity for water than has soap. Therefore the salt takes the water and causes the soap to separate and rise on the surface of the lye in a curdy, granulated state. The mother liquid or spent lye will contain glycerin, salt and other impurities, but no fat or alkali. Skim off the soap.

TO IMPROVE HARD SOAP

A better quality soap may be made by remelting the product of the first boiling and adding more fats or oils and lye as needed until the mixture has a decided taste of alkali. Then boil the whole until saponification is complete.

If pure grained fat and good white lye are used the resulting product will be a pure, white, hard soap that will be suitable for all household purposes. The time required for this final step will depend on the strength of the lye, but usually from two to four hours of boiling is necessary.

TO PACK AND PRESERVE HARD SOAP

When hard soap has saponified pour the honey-thick mixture into molds or shallow wooden boxes, over which loose pieces of cloth have been placed to keep the soap from sticking. Or soap may be cooled and solidified by pouring it into a washtub or firkin which has been soaked overnight in water. Never pour the soap into an aluminum container. Cover with towels or a throw rug to keep the heat in. Let set two to three days.

When cold the soap may be cut into small bars with a smooth, hard cord or a fine wire. A knife may be used but it chips the soap. Now pack the bars loosely, corncob fashion,

19

so air will circulate freely, on slat shelves in a cool, dry place to season and become thoroughly dry and hard.

Be careful! Uncured or "green" soap is almost as caustic as wet lye. Wear rubber gloves when handling the hardened soap until it has been aged a few weeks.

HARD SOAP RECIPES

SIMPLE KITCHEN SOAP

Dissolve 1 can commercial lye in 5 cups cold water. The union of lye and water generates great heat, so be careful not to splash it on your skin. Stir until dissolved. Cool to 80 degrees. Meanwhile mix 2 tablespoons each powdered borax and liquid ammonia in ½ cup water. Melt 6 pounds clarified grease, strain and cool to body temperature. Pour the warm grease into the lye water and beat the mass with an egg beater, gradually adding the borax and ammonia mixture. Stir until a complete emulsion is formed, about 10 to 15 minutes. Pour into a mold to cool.

OR

Melt 5½ pounds grease and strain through a coarse cloth. Allow the grease to cool, but before it hardens add 1 can commercial lye dissolved in 3 pints cold water. Stir vigorously until the mixture thickens. Let stand five to six days in molds.

BOILED HARD WHITE SOAP

Dissolve 1 pound potash lye in 1 gallon cold water. Let mixture stand overnight, then pour the clear liquid into a second gallon of boiling water and bring it to a boil. Pour in a thin stream 4 pounds melted fat heated to the boiling point. Stir constantly until an emulsion is formed. Simmer four to six hours, then add another gallon of hot water in which is dissolved 1 cup salt. To test for doneness, lift some of the mixture on a cold knife blade. If it is ropy and clear and cools quickly, the mixture is saponified. This makes about 25 pounds white soap.

OR

Dissolve 1 pound potash in 10 quarts cold water. Add slowly 3 pounds melted grease, heat, stirring constantly. Add ½ pound borax. Boil and stir until saponified. This takes four to five hours.

OR

Dissolve 1 pound potash in 2 quarts cold water. Heat, add 5 pounds melted grease, stirring constantly. Let stand 24 hours. Add 1 gallon boiling water, set over low heat and boil and stir until saponified.

OR

To 15 pounds melted lard or suet add slowly 6 gallons lye water. Boil slowly over low heat, stirring. To test for doneness take out a little and allow to cool. If no grease rises to the top and liquid hardens it is done. If grease rises add lye and boil longer. When done add 3 quarts salt and boil up again, then remove from heat. Pour into molds.

BOILED KITCHEN SOAP

Dissolve 2½ pounds commercial lye in 5 quarts cold water, stirring carefully so as not to splash. Cool slightly, then add 10 pounds tallow. Bring to a boil over low heat and boil, stirring, until it saponifies. Pour into molds and let set one week before turning out. This soap should be aged three to four weeks before using. It is best after several months.

BABBIT'S PREMIUM SOAP

To make about 100 pounds of soap, mix 5 gallons lye water in 5 gallons soft water and bring to a boil. Boil ½ hour. Then add 5 pounds tallow, 1 pound potash, 2 pounds sal soda, ½ pound resin, 1 pint salt and 1 pint ammonia. Boil until it saponifies, stirring constantly. Pour into molds.

SODA SOAP RECIPES

Dissolve 3 pounds sal soda in 1½ gallons soft water. Slake separately in a stone vessel 2 pounds fresh quicklime in 2 quarts soft water. Stir to the consistency of cream. Bring the soda solution to a boil, pour in the slaked lime in a thin stream, let the mixture boil up well, remove from fire and let stand overnight to settle.

Carefully pour the clear liquid into another pot so as not to disturb the sediment. Discard sediment. Melt 3 pounds grease with a little water and add 4 ounces borax. Pour in the soda lye in a thin stream, stirring constantly. Boil until saponified.

OR

Dissolve 6 pounds sal soda in 2½ gallons soft water and, in separate vessel, slake 1 pound fresh quicklime in 2 quarts soft water. Bring the soda solution to a boil, pour in the lime in a thin stream. Let stand overnight. Pour off the clear soda lye.

Dissolve 6 pounds grease in the soap kettle. Pour in the soda lye in a thin stream and boil until saponified.

OR

Slake 3 pounds fresh quicklime with 3 quarts water. Dissolve 3 pounds sal soda in 2 gallons water. Mix these ingredients in a tub or wash boiler. Add 2 gallons boiling water, stirring vigorously. When the sediment has settled, pour off the clear liquid into the soap kettle and add 2 pounds melted grease, pouring in a thin stream and stirring vigorously. Add 2 ounces borax. Boil slowly for 10 to 15 minutes. The mixture should become thick and stringy.

OR

Dissolve 4 bars shaved yellow soap in 2 gallons soft water. Add 2 pounds sal soda and 4 ounces borax. Boil and stir vigorously until the ingredients are thoroughly incorporated. Pour the soap into a wooden tub previously soaked in water. Just before it sets, add 1½ ounces liquid ammonia, stirring thoroughly. Allow three or four days to harden. Cut in bars, pack and cure.

LABOR-SAVING SOAP

Dissolve 2 pounds soda lye and 2 pounds yellow bar soap (cut in thin slices) in 10 quarts water. Boil two hours, then strain. Clothes soaked overnight in a solution using this soap need no rubbing. Merely rinse them out and they will be clean and white.

SPECIAL SOAPS

ROSIN SOAP Dissolve 6 pounds sal soda and 6 pounds quicklime in 10 quarts water. Boil 20 to 30 minutes. Remove from heat and allow sediment to settle. Draw off clear soda lye, bring it to a boil and add 1 pound powdered rosin and 7 pounds melted fat. Boil until saponified, about 30 minutes.

ENGLISH BAR SOAP Take 1 gallon soft water, 1 pound stone (ground or agricultural) lime, 3¼ pounds sal soda, 1 ounce borax, 2½ pounds tallow, 1¾ pounds pulverized rosin and 1 ounce beeswax. Bring the water to a boil, then gradually add the lime and soda, stirring vigorously. Add the borax. Boil and stir until dissolved. Pour in the melted tallow in a thin stream, stirring constantly. Add the rosin and beeswax. Boil and stir until it thickens. Cool in molds.

GERMAN SOAP Use 2 pounds sal soda and 8 ounces stone (ground or agricultural) lime with 2 quarts soft water. Mix together, boil, settle and pour off the clear lye. Melt separately 1 pound of tallow, 14 ounces rosin and 2 ounces palm oil. Bring the clear lye to a boil and add gradually the other ingredients. Mix, stir and boil until saponified, 20 to 30 minutes.

COCONUT OIL SOAP

Saponify over low heat in a jar placed in a double boiler, 1 pound coconut oil with ½ pound caustic soda. Stir constantly. Add ½ pound hot white spirits of turpentine. Simmer over low heat three or four hours. When clear add 1 pound beef liver gall. Now add 1 to 2 pounds shaved castile soap, stirring until the mixture is of the consistency of dough. Cool in molds.

Other vegetable oil soaps may be made from castor oil and palm oil. The palm oil has a strong yellow color and an agreeable odor. It is often used to give scent and a transparency to yellow soap.

ALMOND SOAP

Almond oil may be saponified with caustic soda by a process similar to that of making other hard soaps. About 1¼ pounds caustic soda will be required to saponify 7 pounds almond oil. Mix the soda lye and almond oil gradually, boiling hot. Boil and stir until saponified.

TRANSPARENT SOAP

Any good white neutral (neither alkaline nor acid) soap may be made transparent by reducing it to shavings, adding one-half its volume of alcohol and setting the mixture in a warm place until the soap is dissolved. When allowed to cool, the soap has somewhat the appearance of rock candy. It may be perfumed as desired.

OR

Shave 24 ounces good hard yellow soap and add 1 pint of alcohol. Simmer over low heat until dissolved. Remove from heat and add 1 ounce almond essence. Beat with an

egg beater to make an emulsion. Pour into molds to cool.
OR

Slice 6 pounds bar soap into thin shavings and put in a brass or copper kettle. Add 2 quarts rubbing alcohol and heat gradually over low heat, stirring until soap is dissolved. Add 1 ounce of sassafras and stir until mixed. Pour into molds 1½ inches deep. When cold cut into bars.

ERASIVE SOAP

Cut 2 pounds of castile soap in thin slices. Dissolve in ½ pint cool water. Add ½ pound potash. Boil until it is thick enough to mold into cakes. Add ½ ounce alcohol and ½ ounce camphor. Pour into molds.

COSMETIC SOAP

Grate 1 pound castile soap. Dissolve over low heat in a small amount of water — enough to make a smooth paste. Beat with a spoon or egg beater, then thicken with a small amount of cornmeal. Keep in small jars with the lids tightly covered.
OR

Any neutral hard white soap may be used as a foundation for toilet soap by shaving the soap thin or running it through a meat grinder. Melt in a double boiler with rose water, orange blossom water or other distilled water to the proportion of 6 pounds soap to 1 pint rose or orange blossom water. Add 2 ounces salt. Boil down, allow to cool and cut into squares.

HONEY SOAP

Shave and melt in a double boiler 2 pounds yellow soap. Add 4 ounces palm oil, 4 ounces honey and 1 ounce oil of cinnamon or other perfume. Boil 10 minutes. While cooling stir vigorously with an egg beater to emulsify ingredients. Cool. It is ready for use as soon as hardened.

BORAX SOAP Dissolve 3 ounces borax in 2 quarts boiling water. Shave 2 pounds pure white hard soap and add. Stir and simmer over low heat until ingredients are thoroughly melted and mixed. When cold, soap is ready for use.

OATMEAL OR CORNMEAL SOAPS Grandmother believed oatmeal and cornmeal made the skin smooth, soft and white. In summer she mixed 2 cups cornmeal with 2 tablespoons powdered borax and used it as a skin cleanser.

OR

Shave 12 ounces neutral white hard soap. Add enough water to keep it from sticking, and melt over low heat. Stir in 4 ounces cornmeal and perfume as desired.

OR

Melt together 12 ounces hard white soap, 5 ounces palm soap and 3 ounces coconut oil soap. Add 3 ounces oatmeal or wheat bran. Mix over low heat. Remove from heat and mix thoroughly with egg beater to make a complete emulsion. It is ready for use when cold and dry.

OR

Cut fine 1 pound castile or other hard white soap. Add enough water to prevent it from sticking and melt over low heat. Stir while melting to make a thick, smooth paste. Put in a bowl to cool. Perfume with any oil or perfumed water, incorporating it with an egg beater. Stir in cornmeal until the paste thickens. Must be kept in a covered container, as it will spoil if exposed to air.

PERFUMED SOAPS

Soaps may be perfumed by adding a few drops of any essential oil or a proportionately larger quantity of essences or perfumed distilled waters to the saponified mass while cooling, but before hard soap has become cool enough to set. If perfumes are added while the soap is too hot they tend to volatilize and escape with the steam. If the soap is too cold they cannot be readily incorporated.

Ordinary soap may be perfumed by cutting it with alcohol and adding the perfume before the mixture hardens, or by melting the soap in a small quantity of water, adding the perfume and evaporating the excess of water over low heat in a double boiler. Or the soap may be reduced to shavings, moistened slightly with distilled water and the perfume incorporated by kneading or by the use of a mortar and pestle.

PERFUMED SOAP RECIPES

SANDALWOOD SOAP

To 7 pounds neutral soap add 2 ounces attar of bergamot and 7 ounces attar of sandalwood.

ROSE SOAP

To 30 pounds castile soap add 20 pounds tallow soap. Melt in enough water to keep from sticking. Add 3 ounces attar of rose, 1 ounce essence of cinnamon, 2½ ounces essence of bergamot, 1½ ounces vermillion and 1 ounce essence of cloves.

MUSK SOAP

Dissolve 50 pounds tallow soap in 1 quart water. Cool. Add 4 ounces powdered cloves and 3½ ounces each of bergamot and musk. Mix well and pour into molds.

BOUQUET SOAP

Sliver 30 pounds tallow soap and melt in 2 cups water. When cooled add 4 ounces essence of bergamot, 1 ounce each of oils of cloves, sassafras and thyme. Pour into molds.

BITTER ALMOND SOAP

In 1 quart of water dissolve 50 pounds tallow soap. Cool slightly, then add 10 ounces essence of bitter almonds. Mix thoroughly and pour into molds.

CINNAMON SOAP

Shave 50 pounds tallow soap and melt over low heat in 1 quart water. Cool. Add 7 ounces oil of cinnamon and 1 ounce each of essences of sassafras and bergamot. Mix. Add 1 pound finely powdered yellow ochre. Mix well and pour into molds.

OR

Add 20 pounds palm oil soap to 30 pounds tallow soap, 1 quart water, 7 ounces essence of cinnamon, 2 ounces essence of bergamot and 1 ounce essence of sassafras. Stir in yellow ochre to color.

CITRON SOAP

To 6 ounces neutral soap add ¾ pound attar of citron, ½ ounce verbena (lemon oil), 4 ounces attar of bergamot and 2 ounces attar of lemon.

BAYBERRY SOAP

Dissolve 3½ ounces white potash in 1 pint water. Add 1 pound melted bayberry tallow. Boil slowly and stir until the mixture saponifies. Add 2 tablespoons cold water containing a pinch of salt. Boil five or six minutes. Remove from heat and cool. Before it sets, perfume by adding 5 or 6 drops of any essence or oils. This soap should be cured before using.

MEDICATED SOAPS

Many of these recipes are oddities today, and some of the ingredients are rarely found.

CAMPHOR SOAP

Dissolve 1 pound neutral hard white soap in 1 cup boiling water. Continue boiling over low heat until soap is the consistency of butter. Add 6 ounces olive oil mixed with 1 ounce camphorated oil. Take from heat and beat with egg beater until a complete emulsion forms. Use to clean scratches.

SULFUR SOAP

Shave 2 ounces soft soap and add ¼ ounce Flowers of Sulfur. Perfume and color as desired. Mix ingredients thoroughly in earthenware bowl.

IODINE SOAP

Dissolve 1 pound white castile soap shaved fine in 3 ounces distilled water or rose water. Add 1 ounce tincture of iodine. Put in double boiler, melt and mix by stirring.

JUNIPER TAR SOAP

Dissolve 4 ounces tar in 1 pound almond oil or olive oil. Heat in double boiler and gradually add weak soda lye, stirring constantly until saponification takes place. This soap is to be applied at night and washed away next morning.

CARBOLIC ACID SOAP
Take 5 pounds fresh coconut oil soap, melt and add 5 ounces alcohol, 3 ounces carbolic acid, 1 ounce caustic potash and ½ ounce almond oil. Stir until ingredients are thoroughly incorporated. Cool in molds.

CHLORINE SOAP
Shave 11 ounces castile soap. Dry in a warm oven and reduce to a powder. Add 1 ounce fresh dry chloride of lime. Add a sufficient quantity of alcohol to cut this mixture and reduce it to the consistency of dough. This soap must be kept in a glass jar with a tight fitting lid. It is a disinfectant and is said to remove stains from the skin.

ARSENIC SOAP
Mix 12 ounces carbonate of potash with 4 ounces each white arsenic, white soap and air-slaked lime with sufficient water to reduce it to the required consistency. This soap is poisonous and should be labeled accordingly and kept out of the reach of children.

B E W A R E !

MAKING CANDLES

"A candle often is referred to as a symbol of the past, yet the candle industry in the United States is greater at present than it has ever been in the past and is increasing rapidly from year to year. Professor Thompson, a celebrated electrician, declares that if the electric light had existed for centuries and the candle was newly invented, it would be hailed as one of the greatest discoveries of the ages, being entirely self-contained, cheap and portable and requiring no accessories in the way of chimneys or shades."

That paragraph sounds like something from last month's hobby magazine, but it was written more than 65 years ago. It shows the new popularity in candles and candlemaking isn't a passing fad. Americans always have loved candles, and with good reason. They are self-contained, cheap and portable. They make welcome gifts, help decorate the home and lend a romantic, elegant touch to a so-so dinner table.

They're also very easy to make at home. You don't need an expensive kit, fancy molds or even special wicks. You still can make candles the way your great-grandmother made them — with what you have on hand. Here's how:

YOU'LL
NEED **A Container** — for melting the wax, tallow or paraffin. You'll need one large enough to hold a batch and heavy enough to keep it from burning. A kettle with a pouring spout is handy and a double boiler arrangement for the pots is essential for safety. Since wax and paraffin are difficult to remove once they are hardened, a container used just for this purpose is best. A large, restaurant-size tin can bent on one side to form a spout and placed in a large deep pan with an inch or two of water is one good, cheap solution. If you plan to make candles often, you might want to invest in a campfire-type enameled coffee pot with an open spout. Between candlemaking sessions, toss your candle nubs in the container for remelting.

Cheesecloth — for straining.

Long-Handled Spoon — long enough to reach the bottom of the container. Metal is best.

Molds — available in your kitchen or at the town dump. See "To Mold Candles".

Wicks — cotton string, cord or whatever you have on hand.

Tallow, Wax or Paraffin — tallow is free, wax is expensive and paraffin is about 20 cents a pound. Take your pick.

THE METHODS

Homemade candles can be made from tallow (the hard fat of beef or mutton), from the substance known as stearin (which is derived from tallow), from wax or paraffin.

Wax candles usually are rolled, tallow candles may be dipped or molded, paraffin candles usually are molded.

Molded Candles — Molds may be anything you have on hand, from a flat ashtray to a tall milk carton. There is no required shape for a candle. If you're feeling creative, you can be as imaginative as you like with molds. If you simply need a light, pour your candle in a cup and carry it by the cup handle. Make it as simple or as elaborate as you wish.

Dipped Candles — The real, old-fashioned kind the Pilgrims made take more time but are much more traditional. They're made by dipping wicks, singly or several at a time on a frame, in hot wax or tallow. The wicks are immersed in the melted substance, removed to cool and dipped again and again to add one layer at a time until the candle is thick enough.

Rolled Candles — Rolled candles are made by pouring melted wax on the wicks in a thin layer, allowing it to partially set, then rolling the wax around the wick by hand while the wax is still warm.

MAKING THE WICK

The first step in making the candle is to make the wick. They can be made from any kind of cotton string or cord twisted or braided together to make the wick thick enough for the candle. The cord then is soaked in one of the following:

1. Turpentine.

2. Two ounces borax, 1 ounce chloride of lime, 1 ounce chloride of ammonia and 1 ounce saltpeter, dissolved in 3 quarts water.

3. ½ pound lime and 2 ounces saltpeter dissolved in 1 gallon of water.

Soak the wicks in one of these solutions 15 to 20 minutes, then dry in the sunshine before using.

TALLOW CANDLES

Tallow is the rendered fat of animals, and almost any kind of tallow may be used for candles although beef tallow makes the hardest and slowest burning. In addition beef tallow is an attractive, creamy-white color with a nice luster and a clean odor.

Since it is not used for lard beef fat also is the cheapest and easiest fat to obtain. It often is available free for the asking at your local butcher shop or rendering plant. Just ask if you can have the beef scraps and be willing to pick them up at their convenience.

When you get the fat scraps home, render them into tallow by cutting them into small pieces and melting them in a large, heavy pan on the kitchen stove or outdoors over an open fire. Keep the heat down low and be patient. If you have a large pan full it may take several hours. Stir once in a while to keep them from sticking. When the bits of fried fat float to the top of the melted tallow, strain the hot fat through a piece of cloth and you're ready to make candles.

And be sure to save those "bits". They're nutritious and delicious. Squeeze all the grease out and you have a beef crackling which is every bit as good as the pork cracklings you buy. If there is too much for snacks, bake them in cornbread or feed them to the chickens. They're a cheap source of protein and chickens relish them.

TO PURIFY TALLOW   Tallow used for candles must be clear-grained, perfectly clean fat. It may be purified by boiling 10 minutes in water, then cooled until the fat solidifies on the surface. The clean

tallow then is lifted off the cold water and dried with a cloth.
OR

Tallow may be boiled in a solution of alum and saltpeter. For each 30 pounds of tallow add 1 pound of alum and 1 pound of saltpeter to the water.
OR

Tallow, beeswax and other ingredients may be melted together with a weak potash or soda lye solution. Let the mixture boil two to three hours, stirring occasionally and straining off impurities that rise to the surface. Chill overnight and lift off the hardened fat.
OR

Dissolve ½ pound alum and ½ pound saltpeter in 1 pint of boiling water. Add 12 ounces beef tallow and simmer over low heat, skimming, for ½ hour. Add 1 cup milk and continue to simmer 15 minutes more. Skim and use for dipping.

MUTTON TALLOW CANDLES

Candles may be made from mutton tallow by mixing 3 parts mutton tallow to 1 part beef tallow. Since these candles are likely to be soft and often turn yellow, the following method of hardening may be used:

Melt the tallow over low heat. When nearly melted, stir in 1 pound alum dissolved in a little hot water for each 5 pounds tallow. Stir until melted.
OR

Melt together 1¼ pounds mutton tallow, 8 ounces beeswax, ½ ounce camphor and 4 ounces alum.

CANDLES FROM LARD

To 10 pounds melted lard add 1 pound alum dissolved in 1 cup boiling water. Boil until all the water is evaporated, then remove at once from the heat. Skim. Use for molded or dipped candles.

OR

Mix 1 pound lard with 7 pounds of beeswax. Melt over low heat and add 1 ounce nitric acid, stirring constantly. Use glass or procelain pot as the acid is highly corrosive.

STEARIN CANDLES

Stearin is the principal fatty acid contained in animal fats. Tallow and other fats also contain glycerin and various impurities. To remove these you'll need 3 ounces slaked lime and 4 ounces sulfuric acid for each 1¼ pounds of tallow.

Melt the tallow in a glass or porcelain-lined container and stir in the lime, boiling over low heat until a thick substance is formed. This is lime soap. Add sulfuric acid and stir until the fat separates. The sulfuric acid will unite with the alum, forming sulphate of lime and water. Cool.

Caution! Sulfuric acid is extremely caustic. Dispose of the waste in a safe place outdoors.

When cooled remove the solid cake of fat and melt over very low heat, stirring to prevent burning, until any remaining water is boiled off.

You now have stearin, a dry, inflammable substance with a pearly luster and no greasy feel. Stearin alone does not make a good candle, but is mixed 1 part wax to 9 parts stearin.

MIXED-WAX CANDLES   Since wax is the most expensive material for candles, an imitation wax candle can be made by melting together two parts wax to one part tallow. This can be used for dipping or molding. These candles look like wax, but the material is much easier to work with.

RUSHLIGHTS   Old-fashioned rushlights may be made by stripping the skin from mature rushes (cat tails) and dipping the pith in melted tallow in the same way candles are dipped. These were once used for household light, but should only be used for outdoor lighting, because the flame is erratic.

TO DIP CANDLES

First cut the wicks to the proper length, then dip them in melted tallow. After the first dipping, roll the wicks between the fingers to thoroughly incorporate the tallow in the wick, then pull the wick straight and allow it to harden.

When hardened the wicks may be attached to a dipping frame (which allows you to dip several candles at once), made of coat hanger wire. Tie the wicks about three inches apart on the frame and make sure all the wicks will fit into the container of tallow.

Melt the tallow over low heat. The best arrangement is to use two pots, one with an inch or two of boiling water, the other inserted inside it, double-boiler fashion. Be sure the container and the tallow are deep enough for the length of candle you want.

Dip the wicks quickly in the melted tallow. You want to add a layer of tallow each time and yet not melt off the previous layers. It works best if the candle is cold, and some people refrigerate or even freeze them between dippings.

When candles are cold and set, immerse again. Continue until candles are of large enough diameter.

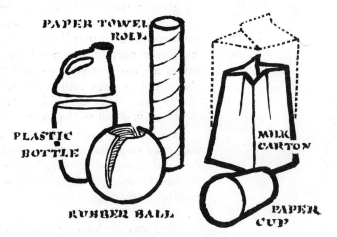

TO MOLD CANDLES

Candle molds are available at almost any variety store or hobby shop but they also are available — free of charge — almost everywhere you look. Milk cartons, paper towel rolls, empty plastic bottles, paper cups and cracked tumblers can be found on any trash pile or city dump. All make great, disposable candle molds.

You can use non-disposable molds if you first make them stick-proof. There are candle sprays and silicone sprays on the market, or you also can use the new skillet sprays which are made of fat. Or you can dust the inside of the greased mold with talcum powder or kitchen flour.

Candles are molded upside-down, with the upper part of the mold corresponding to the bottom of the candle and the lower part of the mold becoming the candle top. Therefore, the bottom of the mold must have a small piece of excess wick. Preferably it will extend out of the mold, but this may not always be possible. If not, the extra, coiled wick can be pulled out of the candle later.

With molds such as paper cups loop one end of the wick over a wire suspended across the top of the mold, then thread the other end into a large darning needle and push the needle through the bottom of the mold, through the middle of the cup.

OR

You may use a long piece of wire inserted in the center of the molds, weiner-on-a-stick fashion, when the molded candles are set but still warm. Allow to cool. When cold, carefully remove the wire and insert wicks in the holes. Stand candles upright, top side up. Holding the wicks up with your fingers, pour enough warm tallow into the hole to hold the wick in place.

OR

The wick may be knotted where it comes out the lower end of the mold to keep it taut. Melted tallow, only hot enough to be easily poured, is poured into the mold until it is filled. The wicks are then pulled tight and the candles allowed to cool. When cold, the candles will have shrunk in the molds. Refill with warm tallow and cool again.

TO ROLL CANDLES

To roll candles the wicks may be suspended on a wire frame as for dipping, then held over the container of melted wax. The wax then is poured over the wicks, and what does not adhere will fall back into the container. The process is continued until the candles are the desired size. They are then rolled, one by one, to the proper shape with the hands, or you may use wooden paddles which have been soaked in water.

OR

Soft, semi-melted wax may be applied to the wicks with the hands and the candles rolled, cut and trimmed.

OR

Lay the wicks about 6 inches apart on a cookie sheet covered with wax paper. Pull them straight. Over them pour wax which is warmed enough to pour but not hot. In a few seconds it will be solid enough to cut and roll into a candle shape. Keep the cookie sheet in a warm oven while you work with each candle.

TO BLEACH CANDLES

Candles may be bleached by exposing them to dew, air and sunshine. If wax candles become soiled they may be cleaned by rubbing them with a piece of flannel cloth dampened slightly with alcohol.

TO LIGHT A CANDLE

Apply the match to the side of the wick, not to the top.

TO PREVENT SPUTTERING

To prevent candles from dripping and sputtering, put them on ice for two or three hours before using — but do not allow the wicks to touch the melting ice. Before lighting, turn the candle upside down and rub a pinch of salt into the wick between thumb and forefinger. Shake off the excess salt so the grains do not fall on the candle. The candle will burn evenly and clearly.

TO CARRY CANDLES

When carrying a lighted candle use a short piece held in the middle of a drinking glass. Let the lighted candle drip for a moment into the bottom of the glass and quickly put the candle bottom on the melted wax to hold it in place. The glass will protect the lighted candle from drafts.

TO BLOW OUT A CANDLE   Hold the candle higher than the mouth and blow it out by an upward instead of downward air current. This will prevent the wick from smoldering.

fJL

CONTENTS
INDEX

NOTES

NOTES

Small white kettle   2#

Large   "   4   3#